ALF®

IN THE ATTIC

Written by Eileen Raycroft
Edited by Martha Kemplin

Designed by Pat Paris
Illustrated by Emilie Kong, Beverly Lazor-Bahr

CHECKERBOARD PRESS ☆ NEW YORK

ISBN 002-689220-0

Gordon's mother, Flo Shumway, switched off the vacuum cleaner. "Gordon, when *are* you going to clean up your room?"

"But hey, the guys and me were just going out to play a game of skleen-ball!" whined Gordon.

"Your room is a disaster, Gordon," said Bob Shumway, Gordon's dad. "You had better do what your mother asks. The forklift is in the garage ready to go. I just gassed it up yesterday."

"That's all you ever want me to do around here," complained Gordon. "Clean your room. Comb your fur. Brush your toes. I get nothing but abuse!" With that, Gordon stomped up the stairs and decided to head for the attic where his parents couldn't find him and he couldn't hear any more orders.

Gordon's mother sighed as she watched Gordon leave the room in a huff. Then she started up the vacuum again. Gordon's dad turned up the TV.

Gordon slammed the door to the attic. He pulled up an old chair and sat down. "Nag, nag, nag! Is that all parents do? I'm just going to sit up here forever where no one will find me," he said to himself. "They'll be sorry they yelled at me! I'll bet they'll miss my face so much, they'll beg me to come back to brighten their day -- *if* they can find me."

Gordon was still very angry at his parents. He was determined to stay up in the attic until they came to their senses and realized a good game of skleenball was more important than a clean room! But soon he got tired of sitting in the dusty old chair, so he looked out the window...

and played cat-in-the-cradle with an old piece of string...

...and looked at his watch. "Hmm, their time is up. Say, I've got a great idea —I'll join a union and go on strike! Lemme see, would that be the Overworked and Underpaid Slave Union Local 93?" Gordon mumbled as he went over to the attic door.

He tried to open the door, but the knob wouldn't turn. "Well, this is embarrassing," said Gordon. "This wouldn't happen to a Teamster! Help! Help!" he yelled. "Somebody let me outta here!"

But nobody downstairs could hear him.

"Ugh! Ugh!" Gordon grunted
as he tugged and pulled at the doorknob.
Suddenly, just as he gave a big tug
the knob came right out of the door!
Gordon tumbled across the room.
"Well, this is just great! I've got to stop
working out twice a year. It's too much—
I don't know my own strength. I amaze
myself. Ha!"

Gordon went back to the attic window and looked out. In the next yard he saw his brother, Curtis, playing skleenball with a group of friends. "No problem!" Gordon said. "Maybe I can get Curtis' attention." He started jumping up and down and waving his arms.

Just then, Curtis happened to look up. "Hey, get a load of that crazy Gordo," Curtis said to his friends. "What's he doing up there, exercising? I thought he only did that twice a year. But, it's about time he started. Last time we played skleenball, all he wanted to do was lay on the bases and call time out for fish fillets."

Soon the boys got tired of watching Gordon jump around at the window and went back to their game.

After a few minutes of frantic waving, Gordon was exhausted and slumped down onto the floor. "That didn't work—I guess I'll have to go to Plan G. Let's see now, what *is* Plan G?" He thought for a moment. "I know, I'll write my own ransom note!"

He found an old broken piece of pencil between the floorboards and a scrap of paper and began to write...

"Now I've got to get the window open so I can throw the note out where someone can find it. C'mon Gordo, you can put the Indestructible Hunk to shame," he said to himself as he tried to open the window. "Ugh, ugghhhh!" he groaned.

Just then, Curtis and his friends happened to glance up at the window again. "That's a pretty strange way to practice weight lifting. Leave it to Gordon," Curtis mumbled as he turned back to the game.

"It's no use," panted Gordon. "It's painted shut. I'm never going to get out of here! And it's all my parents' fault!" he wailed as he leaned against an old trunk.

Gordon started to look around for something else that might help him break out of the attic. "Hey! Maybe there's something in this old trunk I could use!"

He lifted the lid and looked inside. "My baby pictures! And my favorite kitty rattle! Hey, this is neat!" Gordon held up a photo and gazed at it lovingly. "Have you ever seen such an adorable kid? I should have been in diaper ads."

"Ah, yes. Here's the bright child learning how to crawl. Showing a very high degree of intelligence, no doubt," Gordon chuckled. "There's Mom, chasing after me. She never let me just go," he said. "I remember the time I decided to swing on the refrigerator door! How was I supposed to know it would tip over so easily? Boy, did she get upset!"

By now, Curtis and his friends next door had decided it was more fun to watch Gordon's antics than it was to lose a game of skleenball. "Now what's he doing?" cried Curtis. "I don't believe it—he's sucking his thumb! He must have overdone his exercises!"

Back in the attic, Gordon was still going through old photos. He had forgotten he was still locked in. "Yo, an action shot. The kid is sampling some of Mom's spaghetti and catballs, I see. It looks like Dad got in the line of fire there. This picture must have been taken after he took the spaghetti out of his nose. And he's still smiling. I must have been cuter than I thought I was. Ha? I kill me!"

Gordon reached into the trunk and pulled out a musty old Goomer costume and started to try it on. "Ha! I remember Dad dressing up every year as a geeky Goomer. When he thought we were asleep, he slipped foam rubber under our pillows. I always knew it was Dad in the outfit, but I didn't tell. I didn't want to hurt his feelings. I guess it was kind of mean, though, when I dropped a few friends from my ant farm down his Goomer shirt.
Boy, did he jump around!"

"Ha! Here's my bouillabaseball cap and glove," said Gordon as he continued to rummage through the trunk. "I could really smack that fishhead when I was in my prime! But Mom and Dad sure hated it when I stashed a few practice heads around the house for emergencies. Something about the aroma, I recall. Ha!"

"Mom and Dad attended every one of my games, even when there was something good on TV. They were there, cheering me on when I hit my big home run to win the championship bouillabaseball game of the century!"

Meanwhile, Curtis and his friends were already on the telephone. "Be careful when you come to pick him up," Curtis said to the dispatcher from the Waldorf Hysteria. "He's armed and dangerous—with a bouillabaseball bat!" Then they all laughed. It was going to be great fun to see how Gordon would try to explain why he was wearing all those crazy outfits!

"You know," thought Gordon to himself, "Mom always makes my favorite dishes—kitten tetrazini, kitten croakettes, kitty casserole. And Dad's never too busy for a quick game of catch-the-hairball in the backyard. I guess they haven't turned out so bad after all, especially having someone as...interesting...as me around."

Gordon was thinking about his parents and about how good they had been to him all these years. Just then he heard someone come up the attic stairs. He ran over to the door and started to shout, "Help, let me out!" The door swung open wide and in walked his mother.

"Oh, here you are, Gordon. I was worried about you," said his mom with a shocked look as she gazed at the curious outfit her son was wearing. "I wondered where you had gone. And I got the strangest telephone call from the Waldorf Hysteria. They asked if I had a pick up. I said 'no'...but maybe I should call them back. Why are you wearing all those crazy clothes? Are you feeling okay?"

"Hey, I'm okay. No problemo, Mom," replied Gordon. "I, uh, want to apologize for stomping off like that. I'd really be glad to clean up my room. Maybe Dad can help me start up the forklift." Gordon gave his mom a big hug.

"So tell me, Mom," said Gordon as they walked down the stairs together, "what's it like to have an adorable kid like me?"

"I'm just a forklift-drivin' guy
Tryin' to clean my room so's I can see.
Now, just where'd I put that glass of slug juice,
'Cause it's startin' to smell—and it's killin' me!"